MW00487656

Homemaker, on Purpose

How to create and stick with simple routines of homemaking

Shawna Scafe

Copyright © 2020 Shawna Scafe, Simple on Purpose

All rights reserved.

ISBN: 978-0-9952618-2-2

Contents

Welcome

Welcome to Homemaker, on Purpose. The workbook designed to teach you how to create simple home habits that you can build into your life.

Many of us are feeling overwhelmed in our homes. I know I was.

I'm going to share a bit of my story, maybe you can see some of yourself in it.

About seven years ago, I was at home with three small kids under four. I was the stay at home parent to these kiddos which meant I was also the default housewife.....subject to domestic and maternal servitude, *or at least that is what I told myself.*

The laundry mountain was unscalable, the dishes were always multiplying, there were toys scattered throughout the entire house, and I still had to feed all these people in this space! Not to mention the rooms of clutter subtly and constantly nagging my heart that 'I wasn't ever doing enough'.

I could see women on the internet smiling in their well-kept homes with a lack of laundry baskets in their background. *What did they know that I didn't?*

I was met with a lot of overwhelm at where to even start with managing my home.

I was resentful about how much energy it took to constantly maintain.

I was becoming apathetic that this is 'just how it is'.

Soon I was calling myself lazy, undisciplined, and bad at organizing and cleaning.

I started to show up from these emotions.
Because we are motivated by how we feel, so I was behaving in line with feeling resentful and critical of myself and my home.

So, when I felt like this, then I began resent-avoiding the chores. I was letting them pile up almost as a statement of my hard lot in life, like a martyr.

I was telling myself I just didn't know where to start which put the blinders on me to even see where it was possible to get started.

When I told myself how little energy I had then I reasoned that I should be conserving it instead of looking for ways to cultivate it.

And the more I told myself that this was all too much, the more I withdrew from even the simplest way I could tackle the chores.

If you have heard my story you know that things changed when I learned about minimalism.

I can go back to that week in January 2015 when I picked up the *Joy of Less* by Francine Jay and flipped through the pages with a highlighter. I was in awe that I had not realized that all of the STUFF is optional! I could choose another option!!

I had not ever given myself permission to say 'see ya!' to the Basement of Shame, the over-abundance of clothing, and the myth that I had to keep buying me and my kids all.the.things.

So I told my husband I was heading to the basement to declutter, and *"if I don't return in three hours, move on with your life and know you were my greatest love."* And I dramatically went down the stairs to the basement full of neglected boxes and dead air.

It took me a couple of weeks, spending the evenings, to go through this basement and separate out what got to stay and what had to leave. **It was emotionally hard, physically hard, but the long-term results were so darn rewarding.**

One of the hardest things about this decluttering process was admitting to myself the fault I had in all of this.

I had accumulated, I had neglected, I had bemoaned, I had surrendered my control, I had abandoned my privilege and responsibility to be the homemaker of my home.

I had to face the fact that I was on auto-pilot in my whole life, just living on default, letting life happen at me.

So the dramatic descent to the basement was necessary because I returned a different woman.

I was shedding off the layers of apathy and victimhood. I felt empowered and convicted to step into the driver's seat of my life, starting in my own home.

I worked over the years to reclaim my home from the clutter, to set out a vision for what I wanted my home to be, to build into it with love rather than resent.

At the onset my big focus was on decluttering, but I eventually learned that I still needed to build up the skills of chores management. I didn't know it then, but I wanted to build up skills that allowed me to:
- do the dishes without all the mental drama
- trial and error laundry systems rather than feel personally attacked by the ten baskets growing in my basement
- get real with myself on the little amount of time it actually took do the simple routines I said I wanted to create
- become someone who cares for their home out of habit rather than reaction

I was becoming a homemaker of my home. Which to me, has been a lost art. Because we link it to subservience and tedious chores.

Being a homemaker is so much more than its historical role of doing all the domestic chores (and looking good doing it *eye roll*).

Being a homemaker is more than errands and housework.....

Homemaker

- It is cultivating your heart to make your home the place you want it to be.
- It is setting a vision for your home.
- It is knowing what is important to you in how you run your home.
- It is showing up IN your home in line with your own values, rather than sacrificing them in the name of decluttering and chores.
- It is taking ownership over what you want in your home and playing that out in the long game.

This workbook is for the woman who knows that she wants to move from being the victim to being in control of her home and life.

And as many of us know, we know *what* to do, the hard part is DOING it! So I'm here to coach you through that.

Because I believe we are all capable of moving towards the life we want, we just need help on the places we get stuck

And even more, because I believe that home should be a place you love.

Let's do this!

BONUS
Head over to
www.simpleonpurpose.ca/
homemakeronpurposeresources
To get access to the bonus content
guide. It includes books referenced in
this book, related blog posts, and
freebies that can help you with
homemaking, on purpose!

Being a Homemaker, on Purpose

When most of us moms want to reclaim our homes we generally start taking actions like printing cleaning sheets, making chore charts, buying the cute bins to sort things into.

And then, for many of us, this stuff just sits.

This is because we are slapping on solutions without fully examining the problems we want to fix.

We aren't paying attention to the specific stressors of our home, to the things that are worth celebrating in our space, to the ways we have withdrawn from caring for our space, and to the issues unique to our lives that impact how we use our space.

When we aren't paying attention to our life, to our homes, to our feelings, to our habits, then it can be so easy to claim ignorance.

Being a Type 9 on the Enneagram I'm Queen of Avoidance, so I tell you all this with a compassionate pitch that even when it is hard to assess what is really happening, it is also freeing. Because as we become more aware of what is currently happening, then we can know where to focus on making shifts.

Paying attention

Use this space to explore what is currently working well in your home and what needs change:

What is working well in my home?

What isn't working well?

What will my home be like if things keep going as they are?

How do I feel in my home right now?

What do you want?

A mistake that I made early in decluttering was doing it for the sake of doing it - it felt like a chore I had to trudge through. Then when I put my home back together I still wasn't totally happy with it because I wasn't clear on my vision for my space.

I was just going through the motion without using that as momentum to move somewhere meaningful to me.

I needed a vision for my spaces in my home.

A vision is that big idea we have for what we really crave in our life. It is a destination we are working towards. It is exciting because it is just about us and what we really want.

1	**2**	**3**
When you have a vision for your home then chores and decluttering will be more motivating rather than draining.	When you have a vision for your home it is easier to make decisions about decluttering and bringing in new items.	When you have a vision for your home then you have a sense of purpose which will outlast productivity for the sake of being busy.

Set out a vision for your home.

How do you want it to feel? How do I want it to be used by myself, my friends, my family? *(brainstorm all your ideas here. If it helps you, you can also go room by room and then summarize your house vision)*

What are three key points you consider to be top priority in your home vision?

Showing up, on purpose

In my experience of life coaching my clients, I find that moms fall on a spectrum when it comes to their feelings on homemaking.

Some are very anxious, expecting a high standard and offloading their expectations onto the whole family. These moms might label themselves 'perfectionists'.

The other end of the spectrum is a mom who is withdrawn from it, they live in a constant state of overwhelm and helplessness.

I've found it very helpful to learn more about where I land on this spectrum. (The Enneagram can be a very helpful tool in letting you see your stress habits. More info in the resources guide)

And if this feels like a messy topic, or one that gets your back up, then I want to just remind you to have so much grace here. I really believe we are all doing our best. The reality is we largely live and react with autopilot responses more than intentional ones.

The autopilot, how we think and react, has been set over years of our upbringing, our interpretation of what is acceptable, and our views of what should be in our control.

We show up on auto-pilot, but we can also show up on purpose

The way we show up in our messy house can feel justified or can feel like another source of shame - but it is always worth asking ourselves if it is what we *WANT*. **It may be how we've always shown up, but we can actively choose a new way.**

Choosing how you show up will change your personal satisfaction in your own home because you will feel like you are showing up in line with that deeper part of you, your personal values. You will feel more aligned with yourself rather than like you are in a constant take of stress and reactivity.

> Showing up is something you do for YOU, because your values matter to you

How do you want to show up when decluttering is hard and you feel like you are the only one doing it?

How do you want to show up when there are more dishes to do and you want your husband to read your mind and do them without asking?

How do you want to show up when your kids have made a mess and then you have to step in to walk them through the cleaning process?

This will make a world of difference. You can spend all your own energy and time decluttering and cleaning but your house will not FEEL peaceful and warm unless you can still SHOW UP in line with your personal values.

This doesn't mean, 'put on a smile and pretend it is all good that you are doing all the work'.

That is not the answer here.

Choosing how you show up means you strive to behave in ways that are in line with your values, *who you want to be*. And maybe you will see some changes in how you are showing up, like:

- Having conversations with your family from love and kindness rather than nagging and complaining.

- Meeting your kids where they are at and showing up for the messy part of childhood as well as the long game skills of cleaning up.

- Doing the dishes anytime you want to because you choose to (and own it) rather than make it a needless currency of sacrifice and score keeping in your home.

Here are my two top tips for helping you show up in line with your values even when you feel frustrated with your home and the people in it:

Have more proactive conversations.

With your partner, with your kids, with yourself. Discuss things like how you all want to feel in the home, what jobs need to get done, what the benefits are of each person doing a small part, and so on. Remember this is a time to get curious and have fun. Don't make it a heavy, shame-based thing.

Remember this is the long game.

Cleaning skills, and awareness, and routines all take time. So you keep doing your own work to establish this new culture and don't sacrifice your relationship to your family at the cost of instant compliance.

How do you want to show up, on purpose?

How do I currently act (on auto-pilot) when I'm stressed by my home?

How do I WANT to show up, purposefully, in my home?

What values do I see are important to me in how I want to show up? *List 3-5 main ones*

Owning the role of homemaker

If you are like I was, you can probably see the way you have shown up in your home on autopilot.

It can lead to creating spaces that you don't love but feel obliged to maintain.

It can lead to wishing someone would come save you from your home or that you could just move to a new place and start fresh. (Moving to a new house was my solution of choice for a few years, but I see now that I would have still brought me and all of my habits right into a new space too)

Until we decide that we want to be the homemaker of our space, then a home is not being made. At least not the home we deeply crave, and want to be in.

I want to empower you to own the role of homemaker.

It doesn't have to be a label for drudgery and duty, it can be a role you step into out of passion for creating a home you love.

Because homemaking is more than just folding people's laundry. It leans more to creating space and systems for you and your family to function in, use and enjoy.

Really, this includes so much and I can see how the mental burden of all these moving pieces makes homemaking this big heavy overwhelming mountain we don't know how to climb.

I hope to give you the skills that help you slowly build up your homemaking so you can do it with more ease and passion for your home.

The many tasks of homemaking

For the sake of really broadening this definition. I want to share with you some tasks that might be considered 'homemaking':

- Doing and Delegating Chores
- Managing Finances
- Managing Schedules
- Meal Planning
- Meal Preparation
- Home Maintenance
- Appointment Scheduling
- Family Activities
- Home Supplies
- Organization and 'Stuff' Management
- Decorating

Maybe there are some activities that are easier for you and some that you really don't like or have the skills for yet.

You can see that it is almost like running a business, and when we dedicate a bit of time each day to running our home it can become smoother over time.

What is homemaking to you?

So let's redefine homemaker. What do I want the role of homemaker to mean to me?

What do I want to take ownership of in my home?

What tasks do I want to enjoy more?

How will I show up differently when I 'own it'?

If it is helpful for you, make yourself a personal mission statement. Like "I am a homemaker who creates welcoming spaces for my friends and family to gather". Using some values in there like 'welcoming' and 'family' are very powerful.

Simplifying Your Space

Declutter the excess

There is clutter! Things that we don't love, don't use, don't want. We live in a culture of excess and it is so easy to *get things*.

And since we also have brains that tell us not to part with things, even if they aren't of true value to our lives (loss aversion), it is hard to *let go of things*

The clutter creeps in over time and then we realize that our home feels unmanageable. We often turn to blaming ourselves and our family for letting it get this bad.

We live our lives in a home that feels like it is constantly humming with a nagging whisper of all the clutter that needs to be addressed.

I've been there.

Aside from constantly googling 'storage solutions', my main strategy was to banish all the boxes and random crap to the basement and spare rooms. Then shut the door and live with the low level of stress humming through shut doors of these Rooms of Shame and Overwhelm.

Taking action on clutter

There are countless worksheets you can get on how to declutter but here I want to address a few of the deeper core issues I have learned that will empower you to take action.

Decide and do

After doing the work of decluttering, reading all the books, and coaching women on this topic, I believe it comes down to just deciding it is time and just starting. *Even if starting doesn't look 'perfect'.*

You don't have to find the 'right way' and the 'perfect time' you just need to open a drawer and start putting things into a garbage can (trash/ recycle) and box (give away).

Any amount of decluttering you do counts for something. It is clearing space in your home, it is helping you practice the skill (yes it's a skill to develop!) of decluttering, and it is allowing you to add decluttering into your life.

It is a routine, not just a project

You also don't need to find this whole magical week where you can declutter your whole home because decluttering isn't a one and done situation. If you try to make it a one-time, home-cleansing, clean-for-life, event then you will probably be putting it on hold (indefinitely) for the 'perfect time' to get started.

I've learned that decluttering is part of routine home maintenance. Think about how much creeps in - seasonal clothes, socks from random kids visiting, all those loot bag toys, hobbies that have come and gone, jackets you don't wear anymore, appliances you never used, I could go on.

There will always be clutter to be edited out of your home so rather than looking for this magical chunk of time to get started and hope it will be one, and done - look for ways to add it into your routine of living.

I mean, if you can find this big chunk of time to get started decluttering then do that, but don't let it be the only way you let yourself get started.

Getting started will help you build up the skills and habits

Get started with your living room, then your bathroom, then your kitchen, then you will start to realize how freeing it feels and you will get more and more used to making decluttering decisions.

When we cling to the worry that 'it has to be perfect' or 'I have to do it right' then we will never just!get!started!

After all, decluttering is a skill you develop. Like playing basketball or gardening. It takes time, you get better at it, you learn from it, you come to love the benefits of it.

Start with the easiest decisions

When you are first going through your home focus on the 'low hanging fruit' - the stuff you know you want to let go of.

Here is how to know if something is Low Hanging Fruit (LHF): *you don't have to think too hard about whether it belongs in the room/your home.*

It is the garbage in the kitchen, the random toy shrapnel that are under the couch, the paper scraps falling out of the craft drawers, the sunscreen at the patio door, the extra jackets piled up at the front door... (speaking from experience).

The LHF is the stuff in our house that doesn't belong there but accumulates in daily life. Sometimes we don't address it often enough and it becomes part of the landscape (cue the apathy).

Keep your questions simple

There are a lot of ideas on good questions to ask yourself about what to keep and what to let go of. These are great, especially as you do more and more decluttering.

But when you are first starting keep it simple by asking: *Do I love this? Do I use it? Does it support the vision I have for this space?*

When you first start decluttering you are just beginning the editing process - removing the 'meh' and the 'no thank you' - and as you do it over the years your editing gets narrower and narrower and you are now making decisions between 'good' and 'great'. More curious questions might be helpful this far along but they aren't necessary to just get started.

Remember your why

Remember that decluttering your home is something you want to do because it moves you closer to your vision for your space. Keep returning to the vision you have for the space you want to create, and why it is important to you.

If you want some encouragement along the way check out some of the posts in the resource guide at www.simpleonpurpose.ca/homemakeronpurposeresources

Organization that works for you

A mistake I made after decluttering was assuming that
organization would just happen organically and it wasn't
something I needed to foster. After all, decluttering had taught
me that I really didn't have an 'organization problem', I had a
'too much stuff problem'.

However, as the years went on I was feeling like things were
hard to manage. And I realized that organization isn't simply
about putting things in cute containers and bins - it is about
giving something a home that makes sense, *and keeping it in
that home.*

I was making some common mistakes in how I stored my items.
The systems weren't working for me so I wasn't using
them. Then I was feeling like I was a broken homemaker who
couldn't keep her ish together.

It has taken some trial and error to pay attention to how stuff
flows in and through my home and then to create more suitable
homes for things. And it is worth it, it is worth finding systems
that work. It is also important to remember that organized
spaces need maintenance to stay organizing. **The more you use
a space the more maintenance it needs.** (I'm looking at you
pantry, front entrance, kitchen counters!)

Many women email me and ask me what they are doing wrong
because their home doesn't stay tidy. They think they are flawed
or decluttered incorrectly. More often the problem is that we
forget about the maintenance part of it.

What we need to remember is it takes maintenance to *keep*
organized. This means: putting things away, cleaning up what
doesn't belong, decluttering it from time to time, removing old
when you bring in new. Because, after all #welivehere!

Some of the common home organization mistakes:

1

Not decluttering first
We don't need more storage and more places to 'put stuff'. This just moves the clutter around and hides it but rarely deals with it

When you are ready to organize a space, declutter it first. Then you aren't left sorting stuff you don't really want or use into cute bins. Don't organize your clutter. Declutter then organize.

2

Organizing before evaluating
After decluttering you are able to use your space differently. If you don't take time to see how it is best used and laid out you will struggle to make your space work for your organization system rather than your organization system work within the space

Give yourself weeks (maybe months) to observe how you want to use this space. Edit out furniture, refine the layout and then buy the organization solutions

3

Putting too many uses/things in one place
It is not ideal to use one space to store many things, or many different types of things. You end up with a space that is hard to organize and maintain. (Says the mom who used a little kitchen hutch for an office, craft supplies, paper filing, candle storage, batteries, medical records, sunscreen, etc and wondered why I just couldn't stay organized!)

Look for drawers and cupboards you can't seem to keep tidy and ask what should really belong there, is there a better home for it? And if things are used less often, put them into a storage space.

4 Organizing that looks good on Pinterest, but does not work well for you

If we try the systems that others have we often find they don't work for us and how we like to live in our space. When we have a system that doesn't work then we are likely to ditch it and tell ourselves we suck at organizing

When you look at ideas constantly ask yourself what you like and what you don't like about it. Get to know where you like to store things (out of sight, or everything is visible), how you put them away (eg. hook vs hanger, open shelf vs cupboard, basket vs container with lid), how you like to maintain it (portioning into smaller containers, first in - first out) and how you prefer things to be organized (by size, use, colour, enneagram number, date, etc.)

5 Not maintaining it

Organization isn't a set it and forget it. 'Being organized' has two requirements: organizing a space to work for you and keeping it organized. We live here, we use our homes and so that means it requires regular maintenance

Pay attention to the areas that need maintenance and try to add it into your daily/weekly/monthly routines

6 Unmanaged hotspots

Hot spots are places where clutter piles up often (kitchen islands, bedroom dressers, front entrances). These places make us feel defeated about our whole home organization but they are just a cue that we need: a) some peace that these places do get messy, and b) to consider any adjustments we can try

Identify places where clutter often piles up and take note of the common items you see there (it will likely differ by season). Then evaluate ways you can give these items a home that is practical for you

Storing items in places that aren't practical for you

We don't all use our space and items the same, so it makes sense that we would organize different items in places that 'makes sense' for us, but not necessarily for others. (Like when you go to your friend's house and think it is weird she keeps her cutlery in the island and not by the stove)

Organize items where it makes sense for you to get them, use them and put them away. This often means keeping the highest used items in the handiest spots

Not organizing your organizing

A drawer or basket might be a great place to store things, depending on what is in it. If we fill it with a mix of items and the small stuff falls to the bottom and the big stuff tends to pile on top - then the system isn't easy to use or accessible, and we will forget what is in it. (Just look in any 'catch-all' drawer or basket you have in your home)

Look for spaces where items could use some sorting and organizing. For instance, drawer dividers or smaller bins.

Not being adaptable

From these points above you can see that there is value in paying attention to the way you organize - what is working and what is not - and make adjustments as your season changes, as you become more confident, and as your routines are refined

In order to move past the 'I'll never be organized' mentality you have to add in 'I'm learning to be organized'. Keep paying attention, keep trying new things and be adaptable.

Simplifying Your Space

What areas in the home are not working (whether from clutter, lack of organization, lack of maintenance, etc.)?

What are some hurdles that have kept me from tackling these areas?

How will tackling these areas support the vision I have for my home?

What is one area I'm ready to just *get started* in and address the low hanging fruit?

How To Create Simple Home Habits

When I decluttered I just thought my space would alway feel clear and clean, but . . . we still live here.

So it took me some time to accept that I wasn't a crappy homemaker and I didn't 'do decluttering wrong', I just needed some more intentional maintenance.

I needed to accept that we can declutter our space and generally set up the space that we are happy with, but we still need to *maintain* it. If we aren't maintaining it then we inevitably feel defeated by it, and wonder why our home is just so unmanageable.

Hopefully by the time you have rooted yourself in your vision for your space you will feel more motivated to care for it and maintain it, but there still ways we can make this easier for ourselves and put some habits in place so it doesn't all feel so overwhelming.

Why focus on habits and routines?

Often we let our day be ruled by putting out fires, and the to-do list, and the sense of urgency that **everything** is important! And when I coach women on setting priorities in their day I remind them that if '*everything is important, nothing is important*'.

If everything is important, nothing is important

When we live reactively, just responding to the latest chaos and mess, we get really good at panic mode and putting out fires. The more we show up from this space, the more natural this mode of operation becomes. Soon we get frustrated with this hamster wheel of our day and we crave something more purposeful and intentional for ourselves.

It will be an adjustment to stop the panic for a minute and really choose for yourself *what is urgent vs what is important* in your day.

What is urgent vs important?

And habits help you support what is *important* to you. What is important to you in this season?

If you don't know check out the resource guide for episodes on finding your personal values.

Habits and routines allow you to make time for the life you want

Habits and routines don't need to be this big demanding schedule you are bound to each day. Rather, they provide a framework for the tasks that can line you up for a better day.

What do you want more of in your day?
Whether you want more time with your kids when they get home from school, or you want more family dinners together, or you want to spend your weekends doing more fun things rather than chores - having regular routines where you spend a bit of time here and there set you up to do these things with more peace and more preparation.

Something to consider is that you already have habits and routines in place.

Each morning what do you do when you get up? How do you spend your mornings? How do your afternoons go? What are your nights generally like?

You already have habits in place, do you like them?

You might not like your routines, they might not be serving you. You might be spending a lot more time on the perceived 'urgent' rather than the important.

A good way to reframe this is to embrace the idea that you are going to swap out your existing routines for better ones. More on that later.

Clean enough

I am writing you this guide based on how I taught myself to become a tidier person. And I want to caveat that my home is not constantly spotless! After all, I have three small kids and #welivehere *but*, I have become someone who shows up each day to tidy it (without all the mental drama about it and stress over it) because I have done more work on the front end to simplify, organize and show up in line with what I want and who I want to be.

I don't have tips on how to deep clean your tile grout or how to spring clean underneath your fridge. But I do have tips on how to develop the HABITS of doing at least one thing each day that makes your house more clear and fresh (so you can actually spend time enjoying it rather than stress-avoiding it, like I did).

I have built up my homemaking by bringing in one habit at a time. But we don't like the little steps, we want the big whole life change, yesterday! I will never stop encouraging women that small things matter! This allows us to zone in on a habit, master it, then build on it.

What if 100% was not the goal?

I also have found a lot of freedom in doing the 40% instead of the 100%.

So often we tell ourselves that a chore has to look a certain way. It has to be 100%. This is a form of all or nothing thinking. It keeps us sp stuck and feeling overwhelmed by how to get to 100% that we don't even find ways to start at the 10, 20, or 30 percent!

So as you go along, I encourage you to focus on starting where you and showing up for that. Focus on the 10, the 20, the 40%

that you feel ready and able to show up for. And then you can work up to 60, and then 80, and then (if you want to) 100 percent!

I'll tell you some forms this 40% took in my own life. There was a season of my life where I didn't fold dish towels. They got cleaned but I just opened the door and threw them in. There were some seasons where we didn't have rounded meals, just ate random food groups throughout the day. There were seasons where socks were never sorted (that season may have been extended into present day).

There have been ways I give myself the option to do less, just get it done and move on.

Drop the all or nothing thinking and just get started where you are

I think a lot of us moms would appreciate some sparkling tile grout and the satisfaction of knowing our vents have been deep cleaned. **But the idea of doing all that can push us to the other end of the spectrum where nothing gets done.**

Remember, all or nothing thinking sounds noble, we want to strive for the best! But if it keeps us from taking any action and then becomes another chapter in the narration of our life *My Home Is Unmanageable And It's All My Fault* - then it is time to let it go of the 'all' and do the 'something'.

The power of one simple thing

To set up your first simple home habit we are going to pick ONE THING to get started with!

Later in this book we'll talk more about the routines that work in my home and you will outline some that will work for you. But, when we talk about starting with one simple thing you might have some mental lists of All The Things that need to be done and feel like you just need to get there already. You might load up Pinterest, print off the handy charts, and use your willpower to do All The Things - *that could happen.*

But for most of us, it doesn't - at least not long term.

Willpower is finite. It is a muscle that we use until it is exhausted. And then we spend the rest of the time beating ourselves up that we just weren't disciplined enough to get it done. We call ourselves lazy and unmotivated. *We start showing up from this narrative about ourselves and the issue shifts to the 'lack of willpower' we have as a personal flaw.*

There is a lot of research that dispels the myth that *'we just need to be more disciplined'.*

We cannot rely on willpower alone to get us to do All The Things!

Willpower helps us change, but there are many other things that support change. I will unpack them a bit more in this chapter.

When we rely on willpower alone we will run out of steam.
Then It will be a mental battle to pep talk ourselves into taking on all these changes we think we need to make.

So let's start with the foundation of one simple thing.

We are going to start with one thing, because doing one small thing *consistently* can change everything.

After years of trying to create good habits and muscle my way into morning workouts, and daily devos, and salads with my dinner, I felt like I was an inadequate human because I couldn't just make all these changes and have them stick.

So I dialed it back. I gave myself grace. I gave up all or nothing thinking. I honoured the season I was in (three small kids). And this is why I'm so passionate about it. My whole life, health, home, work, relationships, parenting, has been transformed over the years by focussing on doing one simple thing, consistently over time.

> **Doing one simple thing, consistently over time has changed, my whole life**

One simple thing is an investment in your future.
Doing one simple thing builds up and accumulates into something bigger. Like saying one nice thing to your spouse each day, or drinking a glass of water each day, or putting in a load of laundry a day. (A great book on this is *The Compound Effect* by Darren Hardy)

It builds up into making your life easier.
Doing something that feels hard now actually makes your life easier in the long run. As you gain the skills and establish the habit, this simple thing becomes something you are doing on autopilot.

It changes how you view yourself.

I used to dread dishes and avoid them at all costs. I viewed myself as a lazy and undisciplined homemaker. So, as I did the work of doing the dishes each day, I was supporting the view of myself as someone who does the dishes. As we care for our space in little ways, each day, we start to reframe our identity as someone who IS a homemaker.

Starting with one simple thing gets you started.

We all need to get started in order to ever have momentum in our day. Starting small gets you started.

To find a place to get yourself started I recommend using what is called the minimum baseline - the most basic action you could take that would feel silly to say no to.

> Use minimum baseline to
> help you get started

This is how I introduced a dish routine into my life, I told myself to go put away one dish. This is how I get myself working out, I tell myself to go do one push up. This strategy makes the entry requirements too darn easy that once we are there we can gain momentum to take even more action.

Picking your one simple thing

What is one simple thing, that you aren't already doing regularly, that you would like to develop as a home routine?

It is helpful to pick one thing that you will really appreciate having done regularly and makes you feel like you are running your home well. For me, it started with making my bed in the mornings, then once I had that down I moved to vacuuming our living room once every day or two, and then I moved onto doing the dishes each morning and night, and so on.

Six strategies to get started

To get yourself started, let's make a game plan on what it looks like to get started and see it through. I'm going to include some Life Coaching strategies for habit change that I have used myself and with coaching clients.

Time Your Tasks

Think of a task you want to bring into your daily/weekly routines. I want you to do this task and time yourself how long it takes you.

This can be such a powerful tool in task and time awareness because we have a tendency to overestimate how long the small tasks take and underestimate how long the big tasks take.

We need to pay more attention to how long things take us, in order to create more accurate concepts of time for ourselves.

For instance, I was so surprised to learn that it only took me four minutes to unload my dishwasher. I had it in my head that it took

15! And 15 minutes sounded like sufficient amount of time to 'put off' until I 'had more time'.

Four minutes is nothing, and I can remind myself that I'd rather spend it making my home a place I like to be than spend it scrolling a feed of other people in homes that subtly remind me mine is still untidy.

For the past few years I've hosted a challenge called *Simplify For Fall*. It is five days of five simple actions to take in the home. One of those actions is to set a timer for 10 minutes and clear off the surfaces (tables, counters) in the home. I hear so much feedback that the women were so inspired and surprised by how much they could do in ten simple minutes!

Plan out your when and what
To get started with your ONE THING, **outline when you will do it.** Make it a clear commitment to yourself so you can hold yourself accountable.

If it is helpful for you, you can set alarms or visual reminders to yourself that you want to get this habit done.

Then outline what exactly you will do. (Eg. I will spend a half hour decluttering the junk drawer at 1pm. Or, I will fold one basket of laundry after dinner).

Having a plan ahead of time on the task you will do reduces the overwhelm your brain will experience. And we all know that the overwhelm of 'I don't know where to start' will always derail us.

Appreciate what you do well instead of fixate on what you don't
We really don't appreciate ourselves enough for the little changes we are trying to make. Most of us only see all the things that we aren't doing, or are NOT going well.

Whether you put away one dish or every dish, I encourage you to celebrate that you got up to take action.

Fun ways to celebrate and appreciate yourself:
- 'yeah me!' pat on the back,
- post a humble brag on instagram,
- make and drink a hot coffee,
- cross your arms and nod your head while you gloat to yourself in your kitchen (like the moms in cleaning commercials),
- text your bestie (maybe she doesn't care but she's you default accountability partner),
- put on some great music and have a dance party.

Outline what you will do, when you will do it, and how you will celebrate/ appreciate yourself for it

I have three more tips that I have found helpful for me in setting new home routines.

1

Pregame, prepare yourself to get stuff done
When I had a baby and toddler I felt like my whole life was out of control. So I joined a #moms30for30 challenge to get dressed each day for a month (from 30 items I had selected in my closet, I wore 30 items for 30 days).

As the month wrapped up I noticed that I was feeling more in control - of myself at least - not so much in control of these tiny kids who liked to take turns sleeping.

What I also noticed was that if I was dressed myself in any kind of way were I felt pulled togethter then I felt more productive. *(And when we feel productive, we act productive)*

Especially if I had shoes on around the house. This is now my fave hack - putting on 'house sneakers' to make me feel like I'm ready for action. (This may be normal to you, but in Canada we don't wear shoes in the house).

The other thing that I was underrating was the value of nourishing myself with real food and not a stream of coffee and protein bars. Meal planning is a routine that helps me make sure I'm feeding myself each day so I don't turn into a shell of tired anxiety every afternoon.

What would help you feel more prepared to take on the tasks you want to do in your day?

Make it Easier
A mental hurdle that keeps us from action (in all areas of our life) can be something as mundane as not wanting to get up and go get the vacuum cleaner from the cupboard, or bring the laundry up from the basement.

Our brain has a natural desire to stay in whatever state it finds comfortable and making transitions take a lot mental energy. Let's look for ways to make transitions into 'doing the thing' easier by setting up our space to make it easier.

> The more you set up your space to make it easier for you the more likely you are to do the chore.

Here are some ideas on how to make homemaking easier:

- Keep extra cleaning supplies in each of the bathrooms to wipe down as needed
- Keep extra sets of bedsheets very close or in the bedrooms so they can be changed as needed
- Keep out bins for each of the kids in the living room to add their things to throughout the day then they take to their rooms
- Have homes for thing that keep getting in your way at the spot they gather the most (book basket in the living room, bag hooks at the front door, etc.)
- If you like to declutter as you go, have a holding bin at garage door of donations you take to the thrift regularly, have bins of kids clothes in their rooms to toss in clothes they have grown out of
- Declutter your cleaning cupboard to make sure you have supplies on hand that are easy to get to

Start paying attention to the things that need to get done in each space and ask yourself how you could make it easier to get that job done.

Make it Fun(ish)

There are a lot of other things that are more fun than chores. And then some chores that are more preferable than others. I've been known to sort my socks by colour before I enter and deal with a messy kitchen.

Maybe it is because we associate chores with a bad attitude or punishment, but **it took me too long to realize that I could let myself enjoy chores rather than perpetuating my dissatisfaction with them.**

When your kids are small, people tell you to make cleaning a game, to make it fun. Then they won't learn to view chores as a form of discipline and drudgery. And really, we should do this with ourselves more too.

It is difficult to enjoy a task that hasn't been hardwired in the pleasure center of our brain and you are probably rolling your eyes at the notion that '*House work is fun! And magical little birds will fly in through my windows and help me fold laundry and there will be gluten free cupcakes and my hair will look fabulous!*'. I'm not swinging that far, but I've found it helpful to think that, '*this is my life and I want to enjoy my life and so I won't be a victim of my chores anymore*'. So if I can make this part of my life even a bit more enjoyable then I'm up for it.

We don't need to feel like victims to the chores we have in our home

My top way to make chores more enjoyable . . .
Listen to something (usually a podcast or audio book) on wireless headphones. Wireless headphones are such a game changer and you don't need airpods *(though I will tell you to use all of your credit card points to get yourself a pair because they are as awesome as people say)* but I've also had $20 units from the grocery store. I am listening to a podcast 95% of the time, but I also enjoy great music and audio books.

If my kids are home we blare fun music through the house for Saturday Morning Chores.

I like to watch tv or a movie while folding laundry (and maybe treat myself to a glass of whiskey on 'laundry night' that night where I fold all ten baskets of clean laundry that I held hostage in my basement for the week).

I have a mombestie who watches tv on the ipad while cooking dinner, it is her own time where her kids are watching something in the other room.

I will also treat myself to a fun drink like a good coffee or a handful of halloween candy that is still hidden in my office.

Other ways to make it fun are to make it a game: time yourself, set challenges, track your progress. I mean, do we ever outgrow the inner joy of a sticker chart?

But really, you don't have to get falsely excited about any of these things. At the very least consider that they help you pass the time.

Seeing it through (even when you don't feel like it)

Address the overwhelm

In coaching women on decluttering and caring for their homes I find that many of us face this situation. . . .

We decide we feel motivated to tackle a project. We head over to the spot, start to move things around and then decide there's something else we 'need' to get this done. Like a special cleaner to scrub the closet, or a closet system to put everything back in, or some specific bins to sort into.

This is a hurdle of all or nothing thinking. We have 'rules' on how it should be and if it can't be that way, then we won't do it. It is all or nothing, zero or 100.

The other issue we meet here is the overwhelm. When our brain is met with the tasks of breaking down a big job into smaller steps and thinking of alternatives to the all or nothing thinking, it is OVER to the WHELMED.

> Our brain will see overwhelm as a reason to avoid the task

And our brain's response to overwhelm is always 'no thank you, that is too much effort'. Because it is one of our brain's jobs to conserve energy and figuring things out takes mental work.

To address the overwhelm, take more time on the PLANNING end of things.

Write out the steps you think you'll to follow to tackle a project.

Visualize yourself taking action.

And consider where all or nothing thinking is highjacking your action.

- What other cleaners could you use if you don't have the special one?
- What small thing could you get done now if you don't have time to do the big thing?
- What could you use in place of the special bins and closet systems?

Spend more time planning and making decisions ahead of time

The more planning you do up front, the more decisions you make ahead of time, the less overwhelm your brain will have about figuring it all out. You will set yourself up to be more successful.

Willpower and Discomfort

For many of us we rely on willpower to get things done. And when it doesn't work we have this narrative that we just aren't disciplined enough, or we are lazy, or unmotivated. It creates a divide on 'the homemaker we think we are' vs 'the homemaker that everyone-else-who-can-do-it seems to be'.

I want to encourage you to challenge this.

What if we are all in the middle and the way to make change is to remember that willpower is a muscle that we develop over time?

If change has been hard, and getting things done around the house has been touch and go then stop beating yourself up and remember that there are skills we can learn that make this easier.

Skills like resisting the distractions, showing up for ourselves, making a plan, getting started, and generating motivation.

What skills do you need to develop?

Let's make sure to separate who you are as a person from the skills you have yet to develop.

It is our human nature to be motivated by how we feel. We take action (or inaction) based on how we feel. We might feel tired, energized, determined, overwhelmed. We show up from how we feel.

This makes our 'feelings' a very poor source of constant motivation in our life.

When you don't 'feel like it' you can ask yourself 'what now?'

One thing that has opened my eyes to the role of motivation in getting things done is to understand that I won't always feel like it. And decide, 'what now?'.

When I don't feel like, what do I need to remind myself of?
When I don't feel like, how do I want to practice showing up?

I love Mel Robbins tip in *The 5 Second Rule* of counting down from 5 to 0 and then just shooting up and getting it done.

She explains a lot of the science behind this but essentially you are taking action before you brain gets to hijack you with doubts and its desire to just stay comfortable where it is.

Because that's what it comes down to: being uncomfortable.

- Showing up when you would rather dive into your distractions won't hurt you, but it won't be comfortable.
- Getting started isn't impossible, but it isn't comfortable.
- Pushing through won't feel awesome, but it will be worth it.

And I don't mean bullying yourself into it (that is just a form of negative motivation and it will exhaust you). There are mindsets that are more empowering like 'this is hard, and I can do hard things', or 'I'm going to push myself to grow a little bit more today because that is how I develop the muscles'.

Keep looking for ways to use compassion, purpose and focus to motivate yourself in positive and energizing ways.

Because doing the work is worth it!

Showing up for the one thing a day, even when you don't really feel like it will change your view on who you are. Because you are taking action, because you are following through, because you are getting uncomfortable and along the way you are learning the skills it takes to GET STUFF DONE!

Getting started with ONE SIMPLE THING

What ONE THING will I start with?
(eg. dishes)

When will I do it?
(nightly)

What exactly do I want to do?
(unload and load dishwasher, hand wash larger dishes and put out to dry)

How will I intentionally appreciate my hard work?
(light a candle and put in on the counter in the kitchen for some hygge)

What will make it easier?
(dish towels, dish soap handy, bring all the dirty dishes into the kitchen)

What will make it more fun?
(play great music, time myself to see how fast I can do it)

How will getting this one thing done make my life easier/better?
(clear kitchen for the morning, don't have to stare at counters of dishes)

What do I want to remind myself of when I am not motivated?
(it only takes a few minutes)

Building on the One Simple Thing

The gift of done

Let's talk about the GIFT OF DONE.

As you work on the skills of showing up for the one simple thing
you are ready to push yourself again to grow a little bit more.
This is where we can talk about moving from showing up for the
30% to the 60%, to finding the areas where you can give
yourself the gift of 100%

**Because, I'm sad to report that all my extensive internet
research on the magic trick to get you to do housework
comes down to this:** *Do the thing, all the way. Repeat.*

I feel like these were two separate skills I needed to learn.

Do the laundry.....put it away, now.
Bring the mail in.....sort it right now.
Fill a pot up to soak.....just scrub it now and lay it out to dry.

We hijack a lot of our effort when we do things halfway. And while I think we still need to show up, even for the halfway part of things. We can also work just as much on the follow through and give ourselves the gift of done.

Half-done jobs cause mental and physical clutter.

And what is interesting is the other part, completing the chore all the way. generally takes less than a few minutes.
- Put the shoes all the way down to the mudroom.
- Put the random counter clutter into its home.
- Pile up the papers into the filing box and put that in the office.
- Make the bed.
- Clear off the bathroom counter when you are done in the morning.
- Finish it. Done.

Adding in new habits

We have started with one thing. With one chore that you want to give yourself the gift of having done each day.

REMEMBER: You are doing this chore because it makes your life easier in the long run and helps you have more time and energy to pay more attention to the things that matter to you.

As you have built up the skills to create this new habit, use these same steps to bring in new habits until you have the homemaking routine that works for you.

You might choose to bring a new habit in to a place in your day where you really need it. Or you might choose to build on the habits you already have.

Here are a couple of habit building strategies you can try:

Wherever you have an existing routine that is already serving you well, I encourage you to do what is called HABIT CHAINING* also called habit stacking
*coined by SL Scott

This is when you take the occurrence of an existing habit and add an additional simple habit onto it.

This can be very effective at helping you create more positive home routines that help you keep your home how you wish it to be.

> ## Use momentum of existing habits to add in additional ones

The advantage is that you are already showing up and taking a positive action with an existing habit.

In places where it seems reasonable to you, ask what other simple task (even if you start with minimum baseline) could you stack on here.

Here are some of mine:
- I make my bed in the mornings (started by stacking this onto getting dressed). *I added in a quick tidy of laundry on my floor (aka the floordrobe)*
- I do dishes before I make dinner. *I added in a fridge check - I pull out my dinner ingredients and pull out anything that's expired/old leftovers so I can throw those dishes in the dishwasher right away*
- After the kids have a bath, *I wipe down the floors with their old bath towels then toss the towels into the washer*

- When we are clearing up from dinner, *we pull out the lunch containers to pack the kids lunches before the kitchen feels 'closed' for the night*
- When I do the dishes at night *I fill a sink of warm soapy water and wipe down counters and any other big dishes that won't fit in the washer (this one is my newest addition and it makes me feel like a Domestic Maven)*
- The kids and I play games on the living room carpet every so often, *so whenever we're ready to play a game, we (me or them) vacuum first*

Wherever you have an existing routine that is not serving you well, give HABIT SWAPPING a try.

Where you have existing routines but you want to adjust them to be beneficial habits start with swapping out one less beneficial habit for a more beneficial habit.

For instance, instead of scrolling on your phone for a half hour, *switch this for listening to the radio while washing up and packing lunches.*

When you would normally turn on the TV at night, *give yourself a 5 minute tidy and then turn on the tv.*

Swap your distractions for task that make you feel purposeful + proud

The key here is look for swapping out your distractions, that drain you, for tasks that make you feel purposeful or energized.

Routines That Work for You

If you are like most moms who feel overwhelmed by homemaking you have loaded up Pinterest and felt the excitement of new ideas and printables....and then the later disappointment that the printable wasn't even printed let alone put into action.

You aren't alone.

Routines are a proactive way of managing your time and energy

What works for one mom might not work for you. Templates on the internet are a great idea and that is what you should view them as, *IDEAS.*

It is great to get ideas, but you need to pick what you think will best serve you and your home.

There is no life rule that says you have to get up at 5am, put laundry in, run the dishes, exercise, pay some bills, apply a flawless 5 minute face and make a whole30 breakfast.

YES, this can be a powerful routine for those people who DO it, but it doesn't mean you are not capable of finding routines throughout your whole day that are just as powerful.

In these next pages I want to give you *ideas* on home habits and routines, then I want you to make your own ideal list of habits and routines you want to slowly build up to.

Remember - you have routines so that things get done. They are how you keep a baseline of order in your life/home so that when life gets crazy, and other things come onto your to-do list, you don't feel like you are lightyears behind managing the physical chaos of home.

Routines allow you to allocate your time and energy so you can make sure you have enough left for the LIFE you want to have!

It is important to remember that:
1. You aren't locked into any routines for life. Try them out and refine them as you go.
2. You should consider the season of life you are in for how much time and energy you have. Don't overload your list of daily routines with an amount that isn't sustainable (or fun).

Examples of house habits and routines

This is a list of the general habits and routines we have in our home. We have worked up to this over the past nine years and it is what works for us as a family.

DAILY
Morning
- Breakfast, make beds, clothes in hamper
- Clear table, load of dishes
- Load of laundry through
- Take out anything needed for dinner
- Quick pick up (5 minute tidy up)
- Review tasks for today

Afternoon
- After school snacks are prepped
- Bags unpacked and hung up
- Load of dishes
- Sweep
- Laundry collection (scan house for towels, etc.) then put another load through
- Check school forms and homework

Dinner
- Dinner conversation usually includes any plans for the week
- Clean kitchen
- Pack lunches for tomorrow

Evening
- Evening cuddles
- Sweep
- Quick pick up (5 minute tidy up)
- Write down any tasks or reminders for tomorrow

WEEKLY
- Bathrooms clean
- Meal planning
- Calendar planning meeting with spouse
- Fridge clean out (the big clean out is on grocery day)
- Pantry tidy (again, on grocery day)
- Saturday morning chores for kids
- Basement playroom cleaned
- Fold all the clean laundry and everyone helps put away
- Sunday Church and Chill
- Declutter something (a drawer, or closet, or room)

BI-WEEKLY
- Finances checked, bills paid
- All linens washed

MONTHLY
- Recycling to depots
- Items to thrift

SEASONAL
- Closets clean out
- Mudroom cleanout
- File papers that are in a pending folder
- Declutter toys
- Family meeting to set a bucket list and calendar for the season ahead

One other thing we do is declutter things as we go
If it is laying around and it is broken, it gets discarded.
If I'm doing laundry and something isn't worn anymore or is damaged, I declutter it *(in the hand-me down bin in the kid's closet or in the recycle bin in the basement)*

Routines that work for you

Brain dump the homemaking routines you think would serve you and your family:

- Consider the tasks of homemaking: meals, finances, chores, errands, schedules, home maintenance, etc.
- Also consider that not all of these tasks are your responsibility alone, they can be delegated to others in the family.
- And finally, you don't have to do them all at once, this is a big idea list of where you want to go in the long run

DAILY
Morning

Afternoon

Dinner

Evening

WEEKLY

Considering the rhythm of your week (activities and work) list ideas on the routines you could have each day. Note, some people like theme days: laundry day, meal prep day, etc., if that is helpful.

M

T

W

T

F

S

S

BI-WEEKLY

MONTHLY

SEASONALLY

Managing Your Time and Your Day

Most of us who struggle with home management also have this thought that 'we are bad at managing our time', that is why we don't have enough time to do chores.

As you have read through this workbook I hope you see that time is just one other skill that makes homemaking easier, *it isn't the only one.* **And like with all these skills, they aren't WHO you are, they are WHAT you are learning to do.**

But time is an important part of what we can or cannot get done. It is also tricky because it is so easily hijacked and it is a resource we cannot get back.

A misperception of time management is that we think it takes away our time and restricts it. But time management comes down to getting clear on your priorities (your values and vision), giving them a spot to exist (on your calendar) and following through on that. You will feel more satisfied with how you use your time when you align it to your priorities.

Your priorities should be set by your personal values and life vision

This is why it is so important to know your values (who you are, what it important to you) and your vision (where you want to go in your life). Knowing these things act as the filter through which you make decisions on how you spend your resources: your time, your space, your money, your physical and emotional energy.

(Make sure to stop by the link at the beginning of the book for more resources that help you set your vision and values)

The biggest benefit of planning your time is that it allows you to make decisions ahead of time.

The more decisions we make ahead of time the easier our life can be, because then our brain isn't met with overwhelm in the moment of being unsure and having too many choices. Decision fatigue is real and it sets in when we have to make too many decisions in a day. *This is especially evident when it is 4:47pm and you are standing over your kitchen sink eating the crumbs from the chip bag asking yourself what to make for dinner.*

So give yourself the gift of planning some things out in advanced.

The other advantage is that the choice is already made. You don't have to waffle between sitting down to look at the new Instagram Reels or throwing a load of laundry through because you've already planned ahead of time how you want to show up.

Time planning tips

The goal with planning out our time is to ALIGN it with our priorities - to make space for the things that matter and hold ourselves accountable to it.

Every week is practice in aligning how you spend your time with what is important to you in this season of your life

Here are some of my tips I've learned along the way that help with this:

Set a weekly plan

I didn't become a planner until I had three kids and realized that it could make my life easier if I knew what I was doing in a given day/week. Rather than feeling like I was scrambling for control and energy amidst a toddler mutiny of Kids Who Want To Do Something Fun Today.

1. Do a brain dump (take all the things in your brain and put them on paper) of everything you want to happen and things that need to happen this week.
2. Then pull out the calendar. Write down any appointments, any errands, and work/school schedules you want to make sure you do this week.
3. Add in the house habits/routines you have and any that you are working to add into your day.
4. Then consider the natural flow of your day (nap times, school schedules, caffeine intake status) and put in the activities you want to do (alone or as a family).

Morning plan review

A plan is only good if you USE it. So each morning, take a hot minute to put your eyes on it.

When you review it each day cross off or move anything that has become unimportant.

Take this time to note anything you need to prep for yourself to make today work well. *Do you have to pull out something from the freezer for dinner? Do you have to remind kids to pack sports gear? Do you need to put some boxes in your vehicle to take to the thrift?*

Constantly assess your to-do list to note what is truly urgent and important vs not urgent or not important (the Eisenhower Matrix)

Pick one top priority for the day

Highlight the ONE thing you want to make sure you do today.

Just as we have spent the majority of this book on growing in ONE SIMPLE THING - I say ONE thing, because this is where we need to start.

Most of us set out too many to-dos in our day. Then we don't get them done and then we stop trusting ourselves to be someone who can follow a to-do list. Our To-Do list becomes a Didn't-Do list and we add another chapter to our life narration of *My Home Is Unmanagable And It's All My Fault*

Start with one top priority. It gives you excellent practice in setting priorities, showing up for yourself, feeling confident and taking small actions to build up trust with yourself.

Keep some master lists for reference

I know this is majorly nerdy but I love lists. So I would (and still do) write lists in my planner or in the notes app of the things I can do when I find I have some time and I don't want to spend it scrolling through memes on the internet but actually doing something that makes me feel like I am being purposeful with my day.

I found this especially handy when I had all three kids at home. I would write lists of idea on activities I wanted to do with them, things I could declutter when I had a few minutes, snack ideas, books I wanted to read, things I wanted to google that I didn't get a chance to do in the moment (because three toddlers aren't excited when mom is on the phone the whole day), etc.

A solution for procrastination (that you probably won't really like, but it will help)

When it comes to getting things done, we tend to put off the Hard Thing. You know, the project that has some unknowns to it, or some discomfort associated with it. So, we procrastinate taking action, *and then this confirms any notions we hold that we are lazy and not 'action oriented'.*

The interesting thing is that when *do* that Hard Thing we often find ourselves saying 'it wasn't so bad!' or 'it was worth it!'. We might often wish we did it sooner.

> Undone tasks create mental clutter. It is important to declutter our minds, just as much as our spaces!

The best way to prevent this procrastination and regret is to practice doing the Hard Thing first.

This concept is unpacked in Brian Tracy's book, *Eat the Frog*. We spend a lot of our day doing the things we want to do, but maybe don't need to do.

He shares that we should do the Hard Thing we don't want to do, but need to do, FIRST. We should get it out of the way. (Remember, make sure you take a minute to really determine that this is something you feel is really important, we put a lot on our own plates of things that feel urgent but aren't important).

When we do the Hard Thing first then we aren't burdened all day by the low level of mental clutter it takes up in our brain. We get to start our day with momentum, and we get to feel the energy and pride of doing that job for ourselves.

Enjoying your time and your space

As you have gone through this work and developed habits and routines I want to remind you *(again)* that this is all to SUPPORT the life you want. Doing the tasks and the chores allow you to show up and enjoy your people, your time and your space.

> Make sure to slow down and enjoy the space you have cared for and the life you are creating

It is like throwing a party, making the plans, getting the supplies, putting it all together. You want to show up at your own party and enjoy it.

Make sure you take time in your day to do something you enjoy IN your space. Make sure you enjoy your own party.

What it all comes down to

What this all comes down to is showing up for yourself.

We can spend a lot of time researching and grumbling, or we can just pick ONE THING and get started.

Because the reality is that nobody will do it for you.
The reality is this is a gift you give yourself.
The reality is this matters to you, *remember your why.*

These are the lessons I have learned the long way around.

When I knew I wanted to make change it was because I could see that I was letting anxiety take over my motherhood; resent take over my marriage; and apathy of it all kept me feeling helpless.

I have learned the value of caring for things and taking action out of love rather than resentment. Which has changed everything.

When we do things because they matter TO US, we can do them more generously rather than all victim-y. When we can do things because we want to take responsibility we can appreciate ourselves rather than trying to get other people to do it (it is nice when it happens, but that isn't their job).

And finally, when we take care of things and ourselves we get to move more inline with the person we want to be and the life we want to have - *which is what we are all trying to do after all.*

The only thing that you can control in all of this, is how you show up.

About the Authour

Shawna Scafe, also known as Your Nerdy Girlfriend and Life Coach, is the writer of Simple on Purpose, host of the Simple on Purpose podcast, authour of the Life on Purpose Workbook and mom to three cool kids.

She started her adult life with a career in Environmental Health. After having three kids in 3.5 years she decided that daycare was too expensive and that she would stay home and get really good at making waffles and 'saying no to that face'.

Over the years she has grown her blog on minimalism into a place where moms and women of all ages are coming to get ideas and advice on what simple, on purpose can look like in their own lives.

She is a Life Coach who teaches moms how to show up for the lives with more peace, purpose and presence. She provides faith-based coaching and uses tools such as the Enneagram, and the Life on Purpose workbook to help moms grow in awareness, direction and action.

Contact Shawna for comments, questions, Life Coaching inquiries and to send her links to premium cheese coupons at shawna@simpleonpurpose.ca

Don't forget to stop at www.simpleonpurpose.ca/ homemakeronpurposeresources to get your bonus resources

Made in the USA
Middletown, DE
01 December 2022

16539759R00040